The New Sound

By Paul Shipton

Illustrated by Matteo Piana

Activities by Hannah Fish

D1727204

Contents

OXFORD
UNIVERSITY PRESS

Grandpa
Ben and Rosie's grandfather

Alice
Rosie's friend

Aunt Emma
Alice's aunt

Clunk
Grandpa's robot

The New Sound
A rock band

Nick
A singer and guitar player

Imagine!

Now enjoy this story, *The New Sound*.

Chapter One

'Look!' said Alice. 'The train's here!'

Grandpa, Rosie, and Alice were waiting at the train station for Alice's aunt, Emma. Alice's aunt was a very good violin player. She was coming to play with an orchestra in the city.

Clunk had a microphone
in his hand.

'What's that for, Clunk?'
asked Rosie.

'Alice's aunt plays beautiful
music,' said Clunk. 'I'm going to
ask her to play later. Then I can record it.'

Soon they saw Alice's aunt. She was carrying
two bags and a violin case.

Go to page 24 for activities.

Aunt Emma smiled when she saw Alice and her friends. 'It's nice of you to meet me at the train station,' she said. 'Thank you.'

Grandpa picked up one of Aunt Emma's bags. 'I can carry this.'

'And I can carry your violin,' said Alice. She picked up the black violin case.

'Please be careful, Alice!' said Aunt Emma.
'That violin's very old and expensive.'

Alice stopped. 'It's very light, too, Aunt Emma,'
she said.

'Light?' said Aunt Emma. 'Please give me
the case.'

She opened the case quickly.

'Oh no!' she said. 'My beautiful violin ...
It isn't here!'

→ Go to page 26 for activities.

Chapter Two

They looked for the violin, but it wasn't on the train or in the train station office.

'A nice man or woman might find it,' said Aunt Emma. 'I put a note with the violin. It has my phone number on it.'

'Let's go home and wait,' said Grandpa.

Soon they were going home in Grandpa's van.

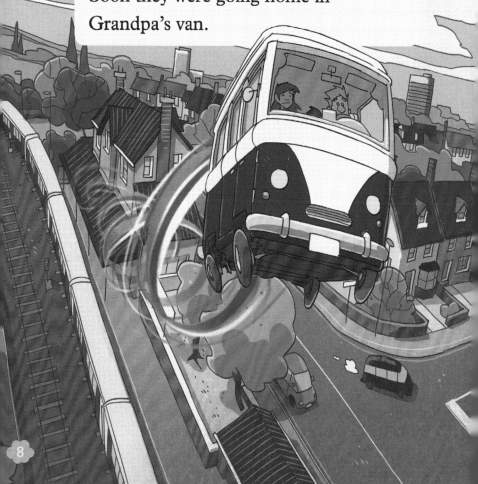

At the house, Aunt Emma's cell phone rang.

'Hello?' she said.

'I have your violin,' said a man's voice. 'Do you want it?'

'Yes, please,' said Aunt Emma.

'OK.' The man laughed. 'But you have to give me lots of money!'

→ Go to page 28 for activities.

'But I don't have lots of money,' said Emma.

'Then say goodbye to your violin!' said the man.
'I'm going to sell it!'

Aunt Emma started to tell Grandpa and the
children about the man on the phone.

Grandpa was thinking. 'Where was this man?'
he asked. 'Did he say?'

'No, he didn't,' said Aunt Emma. 'I'm never going to see my violin again.'

'Wait,' said Alice. 'Clunk, were you using your microphone when Aunt Emma was on her cell phone?'

'Yes,' said Clunk.

'Maybe you recorded the man on the phone,' said Alice.

The robot looked at his microphone. 'Yes,' he said. 'Yes, I did!'

→ Go to page 30 for activities.

Chapter Three

Grandpa, Aunt Emma, and the girls were at Ben's computer. They listened as Ben played the phone call on the computer's speakers.

'You can hear the man's voice easily,' said Ben. 'But listen carefully when I play it again. Can you hear some very quiet music, too?'

'I can hear it,' said Rosie. 'It's a rock band!'

Grandpa pointed at the computer screen. 'Every line is a different sound,' he said. 'Ben, can you take away the sound of the man? Then can you make the sound of the music louder?'

'OK.' Ben's hands moved quickly over the keyboard.

→ Go to page 32 for activities.

When Ben played the phone call again, they could hear the music but not the man's voice.

'Maybe he was listening to the radio,' said Alice.

'No,' said Ben. 'That band's playing the same music again and again. They're practicing. And listen to this …'

The music stopped. Now they could hear a different man's voice.

Again, Ben's hands moved fast over the keyboard. This time they could understand the man's words: 'Soon lots of people are going to know The New Sound's music!'

'The New Sound?' said Aunt Emma.

Ben was looking on the computer. 'It's the name of a rock band,' he said. 'And they're going to play in the city tonight!'

→ Go to page 34 for activities.

Chapter Four

They got into the van, and soon they were outside a small concert hall in the city.

Inside the concert hall there was no crowd, but the band were on the stage. They were practicing a song.

'I don't like this music!' said Aunt Emma. 'It's too loud!'

When Nick, the band's singer and guitar player saw people in the concert hall, he stopped.

'Excuse me,' he said into his microphone. 'The concert starts at eight o'clock.'

Alice started to tell him about Aunt Emma's violin.

'I'm sorry,' said Nick. 'We have guitars and drums, but no violin.'

→ Go to page 36 for activities.

Grandpa, Aunt Emma, and the children started to leave.

Before they went outside, a man came out of an office close to the stage. He saw Aunt Emma, and he stopped.

'Look!' said Rosie. 'He has the violin!'

The man started to run to a door.

'Stop him!' shouted Aunt Emma.

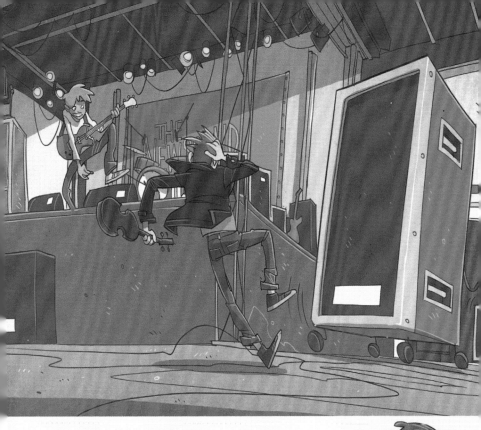

The man was fast, but Nick moved
quickly, too. He played one very
loud sound on his guitar.

The man with the violin was
in front of one of the big
speakers. He stopped and
put his hands to his ears.
The band's drummer
jumped off the stage.

'Give me that violin,'
he said.

➔ Go to page 38 for activities.

Chapter Five

Grandpa phoned the police and soon two police officers came to take the man away.

'He picked up your violin on the train,' a police officer said. 'He came here because he works at the concert hall.'

Aunt Emma was happy to have her violin again.

'Thank you,' she said to the band. 'You really helped me.'

'That's OK.' Nick smiled. 'Maybe you can help us ...'

At eight o'clock that night there were lots of people in the concert hall to see The New Sound.

The band came on stage.

'We're The New Sound,' Nick said. 'And tonight we have a fantastic new player in the band!'

'It's Aunt Emma!' said Alice.

→ Go to page 40 for activities.

The band – and Aunt Emma – started to play the first song. At first Emma wasn't sure about the rock music, but then …

'Look,' said Rosie. 'She's having fun!'

The crowd had fun, too. They loved the music.

'Wow! The New Sound are better with that violin!' said one man. 'Fantastic!'

After the concert, the band were happy.

'Can you play with us again?' Nick asked.

Aunt Emma smiled. 'Yes,' she said, 'when I'm in the city again. But tomorrow I'm going to play *my* favorite music with an orchestra. Would you like to come and listen?'

Go to page 42 for activities.

1 Match.

1 record

2 microphone

3 violin

4 orchestra

5 violin case

6 train station

2 Circle the correct words.

1 Grandpa, Rosie, and Alice were at the
bus / **train** station.

2 They were waiting for Alice's **friend** / **aunt**.

3 Aunt Emma could play the **violin** / **orchestra**.

4 Clunk wanted to **record** / **hear** her playing
beautiful music.

5 Aunt Emma had **three** / **two** bags.

6 Aunt Emma was carrying a violin **bag** / **case**.

3 Complete the sentences.

had ~~waiting~~ record carrying saw coming

1 Grandpa, Rosie and Alice were __waiting__ for Aunt Emma.
2 Aunt Emma was _____ to play with an orchestra.
3 Clunk _____ a microphone.
4 Clunk wanted to _____ Aunt Emma's music.
5 Soon they _____ Aunt Emma.
6 Aunt Emma was _____ two bags.

4 Look at the picture on page 4. Write *yes* or *no*.

1 Clunk has a violin case. __no__
2 Rosie is next to Ben. _____
3 There is a train in the station. _____
4 The train is green. _____
5 There is a cat in the station. _____
6 There are lots of people in the station. _____
7 Clunk is on the train. _____

Talk **What music do you like? Talk to a friend.**

Activities for pages 6–7

1 Write the words.

1 t r a i n

2 _ _ _ _ _ _ _

_ _ _ _

3 _ _ _ _ _ _

4 _ _ _ _ _ _ _ _ _ _

2 Match.

1 Aunt Emma smiled when

2 Grandpa picked up

3 Alice picked up

4 The violin case

one of Aunt Emma's bags.

Aunt Emma's violin case.

was very light.

she saw Alice and her friends.

Talk **Where is Aunt Emma's violin? Tell a friend your ideas.**

3 Choose and write the correct words.

Grandpa, Rosie, and Alice were at the ¹ _train station_ . They were waiting for Alice's aunt, Emma. Aunt Emma could play the ² _____ . She was coming to play in an orchestra in the ³ _____ . Aunt Emma had two bags and her violin case. Grandpa carried a ⁴ _____ , and Alice carried the violin case. The violin case was very ⁵ _____ , so Aunt Emma opened it. The violin wasn't inside!

orchestra

violin

bag

opened

train station

light

city

record

Now tick (✓) the best name for Chapter One.

Aunt Emma comes to stay ☐

Aunt Emma goes home ☐

Aunt Emma has a vacation ☐

1 Choose and write the correct words.

a cell phone   money   a note   ~~an office~~   a van   a voice

1 This is a place where people work.   _an office_

2 This is what you hear when a person speaks.   _____

3 You use this to buy things.   _____

4 You can use this to make a phone call or send a text message.   _____

2 Order the words.

1 wasn't / The / train. / on the / violin

    The violin wasn't on the train.

2 Grandpa's van. / home / they were / Soon / going / in

    _____

3 Aunt Emma's / rang. / house, / cell phone / At the

    _____

4 had / violin. / A / Aunt Emma's / man

    _____

3 Circle the mistakes. Then write the correct words.

1 They looked (at) the violin. _____for_____

2 Aunt Emma had a note with the violin. _____

3 The note had she phone number on it. _____

4 They went home for wait. _____

5 'I have your violin. Are you want it?' _____

6 'You have to give me lot of money!' _____

4 Write yes or no.

1 The violin was in the train station office. _____

2 Aunt Emma put a note with the violin. _____

3 On the note she put her phone number. _____

4 They went home on the train. _____

5 A man came to the house. _____

6 Aunt Emma heard a voice on her phone. _____

7 Aunt Emma doesn't want her violin. _____

Talk What does Aunt Emma do? Tell a friend your ideas.

1 Write the words.

1 _microphone_ i p r o h n c e m o

2 _____ o t o r b

3 _____ h d i l r e c n

4 _____ e l s l

2 Look at pages 10 and 11. Complete the sentences. You can use 1, 2, or 3 words.

1 Aunt Emma __doesn't have lots__ of money.

2 The man was going _____ the violin.

3 Aunt Emma _____ Grandpa about the man.

4 The man _____ where he was.

5 Clunk was _____ when Aunt Emma was on the phone.

6 Clunk _____ the man on the phone.

3 Choose and write the correct words.

They looked for the violin, but it wasn't

¹ ___on___ the train or in the office. They

² _____ home to wait. A man phoned Aunt

Emma's cell phone. The man had Aunt Emma's

violin. He wanted ³ _____ to give him lots of

money. But Aunt Emma doesn't have lots of money.

Clunk was ⁴ _____ his microphone when

Aunt Emma was on the phone. Clunk recorded

⁵ _____ man with his microphone!

1 at ~~on~~ for	**4** used uses using

2 go went gone	**5** a the it

3 she she's her

4 Who said this? Write the names.

1 'I'm never going to see my
   violin again.'   ___Aunt Emma___

2 'Then say goodbye to your violin!' _____

3 'Where was this man?'   _____

4 'Maybe you recorded the man
   on the phone.'   _____

1 Write the words.

> computer screen   ~~rock band~~   sound
> hands   speakers   point

1 _rock band_   2 _____   3 _____

4 _____   5 _____   6 _____

2 Circle the odd one out.

1 computer / (man) / screen

2 sound / music / girls

3 stop / listen / hear

4 music / rock band / cell phone

5 different / quiet / loud

3 Circle the correct answers.

1 Where were Grandpa, Aunt Emma, and the girls?

at the train station   (at Ben's computer)
at the store

2 What did Ben play on the computer's speakers?

some music   the violin   the phone call

3 What could they hear easily?

the man's voice   Clunk's voice
Aunt Emma's voice

4 What did they hear when Ben played it again?

a new voice   quiet music   loud music

5 What was the quiet music?

a violin   a rock band   the man singing

6 What did Grandpa point at?

Clunk   the computer screen   the cell phone

7 What did Grandpa want Ben to stop?

the music   the computer
the sound of the man

Activities for pages 14–15

1 Match.

- **1** talk

- **2** keyboard

- **3** music

- **4** radio

2 Choose the best answers.

1 Ben: Can you hear that?

Rosie: **a** Yes, I can!　**b** Yes, please!

　　　c Yes, I hear!

2 Ben: What is it?

Rosie: **a** It a rock band　**b** That a rock band.

　　　c It's a rock band.

3 Ben: What are they doing?

Rosie: **a** They're practice.　**b** They're practicing.

　　　c They're practiced.

4 Ben: Did you hear their name?

Rosie: **a** I can't.　**b** I didn't.　**c** I haven't.

3 **Order the events in Chapter Three.**

They heard a different man's voice. _____

They heard the man's voice easily. _____

They were all at Ben's computer. _1_

Ben looked for The New Sound on
his computer. _____

They heard the music but not the man's voice. _____

They heard some quiet music, too. _____

Ben found the band's name on his computer. _____

Ben played the phone call on his computer. _____

4 **Circle the correct answer.**

1 What is The New Sound?

    an orchestra   violin players   a rock band

Now tick (✓) the best name for Chapter Three.

The Old Sound ☐

The Big Sound ☐

The New Sound ☐

Talk **What do Grandpa, Aunt Emma, and the children do next? Tell a friend your ideas.**

1 Circle the correct words.

1 They went to a **concert hall / train station** in the city.

2 There was no **band / crowd** in the concert hall.

3 The band were practicing a **violin / song**.

4 Nick was the band's singer and **guitar / drum** player.

5 Alice told the singer about the **computer / violin**.

6 The band didn't have any **guitars / violins**.

2 Match. Then complete the sentences using the past tense.

doesn't	are	get	see	have
got	had	didn't	saw	were

1 They all ____got____ into the van.

2 The band _____ on the stage.

3 Aunt Emma _____ like the music.

4 The singer _____ them in the concert hall.

5 The band _____ guitars but no violin.

3 Order the words.

1 outside / a small / were / concert hall. / They

_____

2 band / practicing / The / song. / a / were

_____

3 concert / at / The / eight o'clock. / started

_____

4 Nick / about / Alice told / violin. / Aunt Emma's

_____

5 band / a / have / The / violin. / didn't

_____

**4 Look at the picture on page 17.
Write _yes_ or _no_.**

1 There are four people on the stage.   _____

2 There are some bags on the stage.   _____

3 The singer has a black hat.   _____

4 The singer has a guitar.   _____

5 Alice is talking to the singer.   _____

6 Grandpa is next to Rosie.   _____

7 Ben has a microphone.   _____

1 **Circle the correct answers.**

1 What did Grandpa, Aunt Emma, and the children do?

stay and watch   start to leave
play the drums

2 Where did a man come from?

the stage   outside   an office

3 What did the man have?

a guitar   Aunt Emma's violin   a computer

4 Where did the man run to?

the band   Grandpa   the door

5 What did Nick do?

ran after the man   called the police
played a sound on his guitar

6 What was the man with the violin in front of?

a speaker   the drums   the door

7 What did the man do?

shouted at Nick   put his hands on his head
put his hands to his ears

2 Choose and write the correct words.

They went to a ¹ _____ in the city. There was no crowd in the hall, but the band were practicing a song. Nick was the band's singer and ² _____ player. The band didn't have any violins. When they were leaving, Rosie saw a man with Aunt Emma's violin. The man started to ³ _____. But Nick played a sound on his guitar. The man put his ⁴ _____ to his ears and the band's drummer jumped off the ⁵ _____ and took the violin.

run

drum

hands

concert hall

crowd

speakers

stage

guitar

Now tick (✓) the best name for Chapter Four.

Meeting Nick ☐   Helping Nick ☐

Finding Nick

1 Write the words.

1 _ _ _ _ _ _ _
  _ _ _ _ _ _ _

2 _ _ _ _ _ _

3 _ _ _ _

4 _ _ _ _ _ _

2 Match.

1 Two police officers	in the band!
2 The man picked up	to help The New Sound.
3 Nick wanted Aunt Emma	took the man away.
4 Aunt Emma was	the violin on the train.

3 Choose and write the correct words.

3

Grandpa phoned ¹ _____ police, and they came to ² _____ the man away. The man picked ³ _____ Aunt Emma's violin on the train. He came to the concert hall ⁴ _____ work. Aunt Emma was ⁵ _____ to have her violin back.

1 a   an   the

2 take   took   taking

3 at   on   up

4 for   of   to

5 happily   happy   happier

4 Complete the sentences.

came   was   see   had

1 People came to _____ The New Sound.

2 The band _____ on stage.

3 That night the band _____ a new player.

4 The new player _____ Aunt Emma!

1 Look at pages 22 and 23. Complete the sentences. You can use 1, 2, or 3 words.

1 They started _____ the first song.

2 Aunt Emma _____ fun!

3 The crowd _____ the music.

4 After the concert, _____ happy.

5 Nick wanted Aunt Emma _____ with them again.

6 Aunt Emma _____ and said, 'Yes.'

2 Circle the mistakes. Then write the correct words.

1 Aunt Emma weren't sure about the rock music.   _____

2 Aunt Emma and the crowd did fun.   _____

3 The band was gooder with a violin.   _____

4 Later the concert, the band were happy.   _____

5 'Can you play with we again?'   _____

6 'Yes, when I'm on the city again.'   _____

7 Tomorrow Aunt Emma is going to play by an orchestra.   _____

3 **Who said this? Write the names from Chapter Five.**

1 'Look. She's having fun!'   _____

2 'He picked up your violin on
the train.'   _____

3 'Tonight we have a fantastic new
player in the band!'   _____

4 'Would you like to come and listen?'   _____

5 'The New Sound are better with
that violin!'   _____

6 'Thank you. You really helped me.'   _____

7 'It's Aunt Emma!'   _____

4 **Order the events in Chapter Five.**

Two police officers took the man away.   _____

The band and Aunt Emma played
the first song.   _____

Aunt Emma was happy to have her violin.   _____

Grandpa phoned the police.   _____

After the concert, the band were happy.   _____

The New Sound came on stage.   _____

Talk **Do you like this story? Talk to a friend.**

My Rock Band!

1 Match the music words.

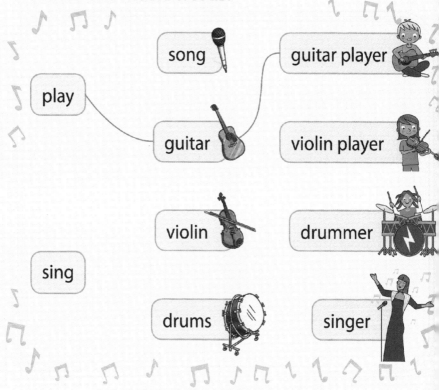

song

play

guitar

guitar player

violin player

violin

drummer

sing

drums

singer

2 Do you know more music words? Write them here.

_____

_____

Talk **Think about a band from your country. What is the name of the band? Tell your friend what you know about the band.**

3 You are going to make a new band. Draw a
picture of your band on stage in a concert hall.

4 Answer the questions about your band.

What is the name of your band?

How many people are in your band?

Who is the singer in your band?

Is there a guitar player in your band?

Is there a drummer in your band?

What other people are in your band?

What music does your band play?

Picture Dictionary

computer
screen

concert
hall

crowd

drum

drummer

expensive

guitar

guitar
player

help

keyboard

light

loud

microphone

music

note

office

 orchestra

 phone call

 police officer

 radio

 record

 ring
past rang

 rock band

 singer

 sound

 speakers

 stage

 train station

 violin

 violin case

 violin player

 voice

Oxford Read and Imagine graded readers are at nine levels (Early Starter, Starter, Beginner, and Levels 1 to 6) for students from age 3 or 4 and older. They offer great stories to read and enjoy.

Activities provide Cambridge Young Learner Exams preparation. See Key below.

At Levels 1 to 6, every storybook reader links to an **Oxford Read and Discover** non-fiction reader, giving students a chance to find out more about the world around them, and an opportunity for Content and Language Integrated Learning (CLIL).

For more information about **Read and Imagine**, and for Teacher's Notes, go to www.oup.com/elt/teacher/readandimagine

Oxford Read and Discover

Do you want to find out more about music, musical instruments, and sound? You can read this non-fiction book.

OXFORD
UNIVERSITY PRESS

Great Clarendon Street, Oxford, OX2 6DP, United Kingdom

Oxford University Press is a department of the University of Oxford. It furthers the University's objective of excellence in research, scholarship, and education by publishing worldwide. Oxford is a registered trade mark of Oxford University Press in the UK and in certain other countries

© Oxford University Press 2015

The moral rights of the author have been asserted

First published in 2015

2019 2018 2017 2016 2015

10 9 8 7 6 5 4 3 2 1

ISBN: 978 0 19 472333 6

Printed in China

This book is printed on paper from certified and well-managed sources

ACKNOWLEDGEMENTS

Main illustrations by: Matteo Piana.

Additional illustrations by: Dusan Pavlic/Beehive Illustrati Alan Rowe, Mark Ruffle.